Smarter Balanced Grade 11 Math Practice

GET DIGITAL ACCESS TO

► Two Performance Tasks (PTs)

► Two Computer Adaptive Tests (CATs)

► Additional Practice Questions

REGISTER NOW

Important Instruction

Register online using the link and the access code provided by your teacher.

Enter the access code (for your reference) in the box given below.

Access Code:

Smarter Balanced Assessments and Online Workbooks: 11th Grade Math, Student Copy

Contributing Author - Paul Spinler
Contributing Author - Karen Russell
Contributing Author - Larry Russel
Executive Producer - Mukunda Krishnaswamy
Designer and Illustrator - Devaraj D

COPYRIGHT ©2020 by Lumos Information Services, LLC. ALL RIGHTS RESERVED. No portion of this book may be reproduced mechanically, electronically or by any other means, including photocopying, recording, taping, Web Distribution or Information Storage and Retrieval systems, without prior written permission of the Publisher, Lumos Information Services, LLC.

NGA Center/CCSSO are the sole owners and developers of the Common Core State Standards, which does not sponsor or endorse this product. © Copyright 2010. National Governors Association Center for Best Practices and Council of Chief State School Officers.

ISBN 13: 978-1729282748

Printed in the United States of America

FOR SCHOOL EDITION AND PERMISSIONS, CONTACT US

LUMOS INFORMATION SERVICES, LLC

PO Box 1575, Piscataway, NJ 08855-1575
www.LumosLearning.com

Email: support@lumoslearning.com
Tel: (732) 384-0146
Fax: (866) 283-6471

Table of Contents

Introduction	1
Practice Test 1	**2**
Performance Task (PT) 1	2
Computer Adaptive Test (CAT) 1	6
Practice Test 2	**20**
Performance Task (PT) 2	20
Computer Adaptive Test (CAT) 2	23
Additional Information	**37**
Test Taking Tips	37

INTRODUCTION

This book is specifically designed to improve student achievement on the Smarter Balanced Assessments (SBA). Students perform at their best on standardized tests when they feel comfortable with the test content as well as the test format.

This Lumos tedBook offers two full-length practice tests, aligned to the common core standards. Taking these tests will help students get a comprehensive review of the standards assessed on the SBA.

On registering, the practice tests can also be accessed online. Lumos online practice tests are meticulously designed to mirror the state assessment. They adhere to the guidelines provided by the state for the number of sessions and questions, standards, difficulty level, question types, test duration, and more.

Additional practice is also available for each standard in the online program. The lessons contain rigorous questions aligned to the state standards. Students will gain proficiency in each grade-level standard by working through these activities.

Student Name: Start Time:
Test Date: End Time:

Here are some reminders for when you are taking the Practice Test.

To answer the questions on the test, use the directions given in the question. If you do not know the answer to a question, skip it and go on to the next question. If time permits, you may return to questions in this session only. Do your best to answer every question.

Practice Test 1
Performance Task (PT) - 1

Special Triangles

Each of the questions show different types of special triangles.
For each of the triangles shown,

1. Identify the type of special triangle
2. Find the length of the missing side and
3. Explain in detail how you arrived at the answer

1. Find the length of side "a" in the figure below. Also identify the type of triangle and explain how you arrived at the answer.

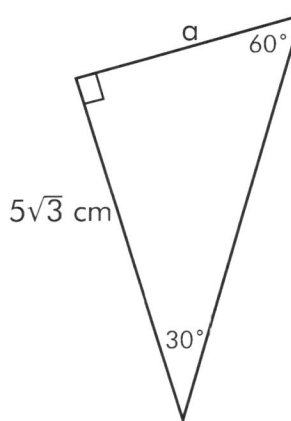

LumosLearning.com

1.1 Find the length of side "y" in the figure below. Also identify the type of triangle and explain how you arrived at the answer.

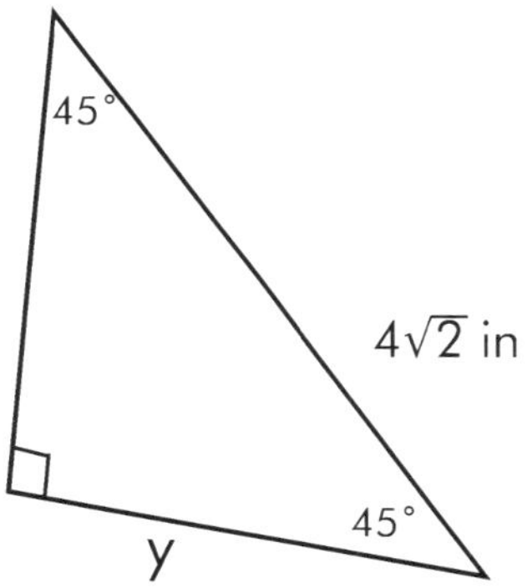

1.2 Find the length of side "s" in the figure below. Also identify the type of triangle and explain how you arrived at the answer.

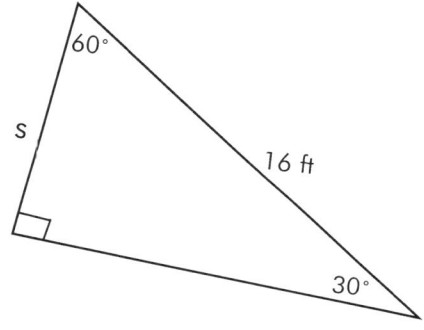

1.3 Find the length of side "a" in the figure below.

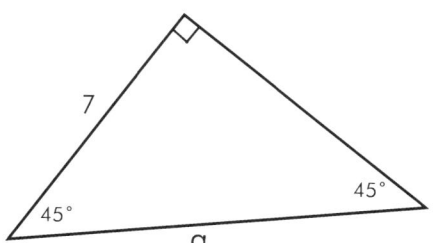

Ⓐ $7\sqrt{2}$
Ⓑ $\sqrt{2}$
Ⓒ 7
Ⓓ $7\sqrt{3}$

1.4 Find the missing side in a special right triangle

Find the length of side p in the figure below.

Answer must be expressed in simplest radical form.

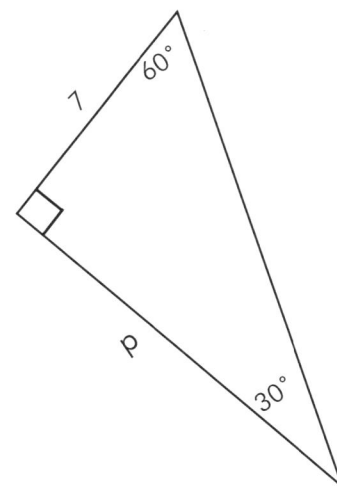

Student Name: **Start Time:**
Test Date: **End Time:**

Here are some reminders for when you are taking the Practice Test.

To answer the questions on the test, use the directions given in the question. If you do not know the answer to a question, skip it and go on to the next question. If time permits, you may return to questions in this session only. Do your best to answer every question.

Computer Adaptive Test (CAT) - 1

1. What is the term with the highest degree in the expression
$3x^2y - 5xy^7 + 8x^4y^5 - 6xy$?

   Ⓐ $3x^2y$
   Ⓑ $-6xy$
   Ⓒ $-5xy^7$
   Ⓓ $8x^4y^5$

2. Which of the following is a zero of the following quadratic expression ?
$6x^2 - 17x - 14$

   Ⓐ   -2

   Ⓑ   7

   Ⓒ $\frac{2}{3}$

   Ⓓ $-\frac{7}{2}$

   Ⓔ $\frac{7}{2}$

3. The sum of three consecutive even integers is 72. What is the middle integer?

   Ⓐ 22
   Ⓑ 26
   Ⓒ 28
   Ⓓ 24

4. A rectangular field has a perimeter of 300m. What is the area of the field if the length of the field is twice the width of the field?

   Ⓐ 5000 m²
   Ⓑ 300 m²
   Ⓒ 5000 m
   Ⓓ 600 m²

5. Suppose the stacks of cases of bottled water on the shelves of a major grocery store follow the graph of the equation $4x + y = 36$ where x is hours after the store opens and y is the number of cases on the shelves. All of the water is sold. What is the domain of the variable x ?

   Ⓐ [0,6]
   Ⓑ [0,9]
   Ⓒ [0,12]
   Ⓓ [-2,9]

6. Solve for b in the formula $A = \frac{1}{2} h(B + b)$

   Ⓐ $b = \frac{1}{2} h(B+A)$

   Ⓑ $b = \frac{1}{2} h(A+b)$

   Ⓒ $b = \frac{2A}{h} - B$

   Ⓓ $b = \frac{2A}{B} - h$

7. What is the first step in solving this equation?
   $4x - 7 = 21$

   Ⓐ Add 7
   Ⓑ Subtract 7
   Ⓒ Multiply by 4
   Ⓓ Divide by 4

8. What is the last step to solve the below equation for x?
$3\sqrt{x} + 4 = 13$

Ⓐ Square the equation
Ⓑ Subtract 4
Ⓒ Multiply by 3
Ⓓ divide by 3

9. Solve: $5x + 7 \geq 32$

Ⓐ $x = 5$
Ⓑ $x \leq 5$
Ⓒ $x \geq 5$
Ⓓ $x > 5$

10. Solve: $4(x-5)+5=21$

Ⓐ 8
Ⓑ 32
Ⓒ 9
Ⓓ 36

11. The graph of $x-3y=-6$ is shown below. What do the points on the graph represent?

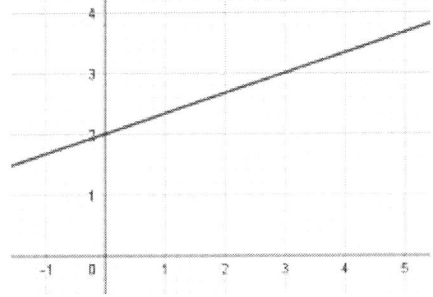

Ⓐ All solutions to the equation
Ⓑ Restrictions on the domain
Ⓒ Output values
Ⓓ Input values

12. The graph of $y = x^2 - 2x - 8$ is shown below. What are the solutions to the curve?

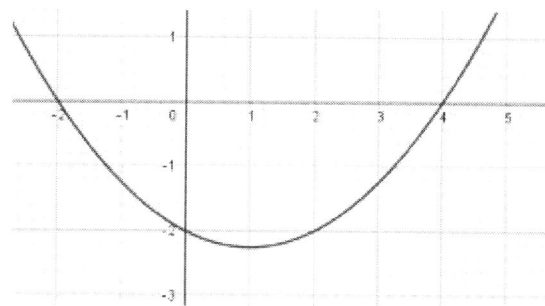

Ⓐ $x = -2, 4$
Ⓑ $y = -2, 4$
Ⓒ $x = -4, 2$
Ⓓ $y = -4, 2$

13. What type of number gets a mathematician in trouble the most when trying to use a function to model a real world situation? Why?

14. Which is the correct graph of y > 2x + 3 ?

Ⓐ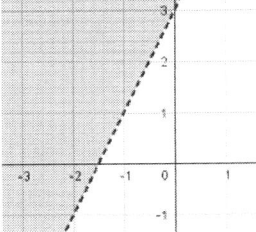

Ⓑ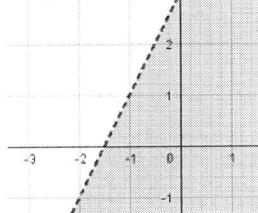

Ⓒ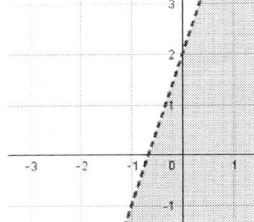

Ⓓ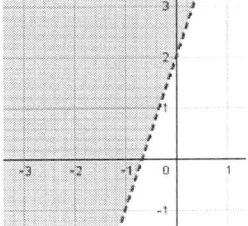

15. Which statement is true about the domain and range of a function?

Ⓐ The domain is the set of outputs, the range is the set of inputs
Ⓑ The domain is the set of inputs, the range is the set of outputs
Ⓒ The range is the set of independent variables, the domain is the set of dependent variables
Ⓓ The domain is the set of independent variables, the range is the also the set of independent variables

16. Which function squares the input variable, then triples that value, adds five times the input variable and then subtracts twelve?

    Ⓐ $f(x) = -3x^2 + 5x - 12$
    Ⓑ $f(x) = 3x^2 + 5x - 12$
    Ⓒ $f(x) = 3x^2 - 5x - 12$
    Ⓓ $f(x) = 3x^2 + 5x + 12$

17. During an Air Show, an acrobatic plane dives toward the ground and then veers upward just above ground level. The path of the parabolic flight is shown below. What does the vertex of the parabolic path represent?

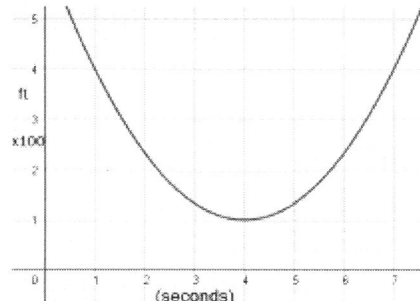

    Ⓐ The plane is at its maximum height of 100 feet above the ground at 4 seconds.
    Ⓑ The plane is at its minimum height of 100 feet above the ground at 4 seconds.
    Ⓒ The plane is at its maximum height of 400 feet above the ground at 1 seconds.
    Ⓓ The plane is at its minimum height of 400 feet above the ground at 1 seconds.

18. The graph of $f(x) = \frac{1}{4}x^3 - x^2 - x + 1$ is shown below. Over which interval is $f(x)$ decreasing?

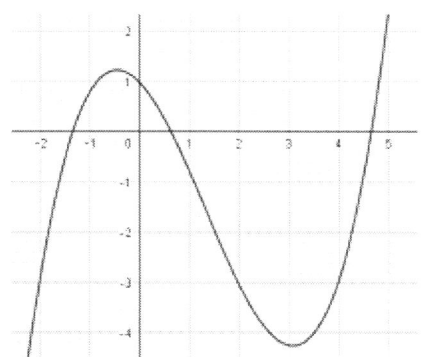

LumosLearning.com

Ⓐ (3.10, ∞)
Ⓑ (-4.26, 1.23)
Ⓒ (-0.43, 3.10)
Ⓓ (-∞, 3. -0.43)

19. **Function h(x)=f(x)+g(x).**
   What is h(x) if $f(x) = x^2 - 3x + 9$ and, $g(x) = 6x^2 - 4x - 7$?

   Ⓐ $h(x) = 7x^2 - 7x + 2$
   Ⓑ $h(x) = 7x^4 - 7x^2 + 2$
   Ⓒ $h(x) = 7x^2 + 7x + 2$
   Ⓓ $h(x) = 7x^2 + 7x + 16$

20. **Write the explicit formula for this arithmetic sequence: $-34, -64, -94, -124, \ldots$**

   Ⓐ $a_n = -30n + 64$
   Ⓑ $a_n = -30n - 64$
   Ⓒ $a_n = 30n - 64$
   Ⓓ $a_n = -30n - 4$

21. **Suppose △ABC ~ △DEF shown below. What is cos F?**

   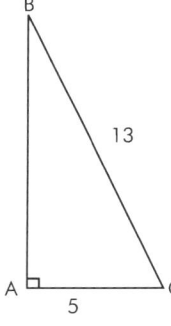

   Ⓐ $\dfrac{13}{5}$

   Ⓑ $\dfrac{12}{13}$

   Ⓒ $\dfrac{13}{12}$

   Ⓓ $\dfrac{5}{13}$

22. Suppose angle B and angle C are the acute angles in △ABC. If cos angle B = $\frac{7}{25}$, what is sin angle C?

Ⓐ $\frac{7}{24}$

Ⓑ $\frac{7}{25}$

Ⓒ $\frac{24}{25}$

Ⓓ $\frac{25}{7}$

23. A survey of 9th and 10th graders was conducted to see which type of pet they preferred. The result of the survey is in the table.

What is the probability that a student prefers a cat, given that the student is a 10th grader?

Grade	Bird	Cat	Dog	Total
9	3	43	50	96
10	7	36	61	104
Total	10	79	111	200

Ⓐ $\frac{79}{200}$

Ⓑ $\frac{43}{96}$

Ⓒ $\frac{43}{200}$

Ⓓ $\frac{9}{26}$

24. Rewrite $\sqrt[4]{12a^3b^4c^5}$ using rational exponents.

Ⓐ $3a^{\frac{3}{4}}bc^{\frac{5}{4}}$

Ⓑ $12^{\frac{1}{4}}a^{\frac{3}{4}}bc^{\frac{5}{4}}$

Ⓒ $12^{\frac{1}{4}}a^3bc^{\frac{4}{5}}$

Ⓓ $12^4a^{12}b^{16}c^{20}$

25. An airplane is flying 800 miles per hour. To the nearest foot, how many feet per second is this?

Ⓐ 70,400
Ⓑ 1,173
Ⓒ 20
Ⓓ 1,111

26. Every month, a group of 36 students writes essays in a writing class. Each student writes 4 essays, and each essay contains an average of 800 words. How many words do the students write each month?

Ⓐ 144,000
Ⓑ 28,800
Ⓒ 3,200
Ⓓ 115,200

27. What is the exponential model for the data in the table below?

x	y
5	160
7	640

Ⓐ $y = 5(2)^x$
Ⓑ $y = 2(5)^x$
Ⓒ $y = 10(2)^x$
Ⓓ $y = 32x$

28. Jack purchased some shares of stock in a successful company. The graph below shows the value of the shares over time. He wants to sell the shares when their value is twice what he paid for them. During which month after Jack bought the shares are the shares double their original value?

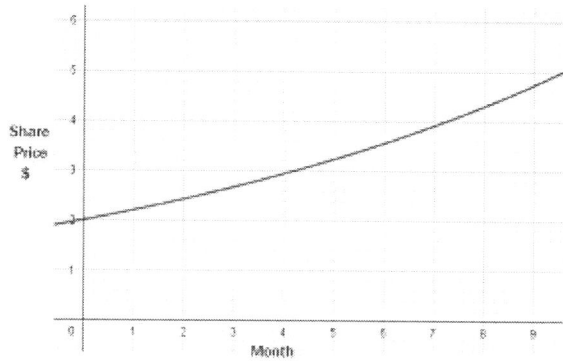

Ⓐ 6
Ⓑ 7
Ⓒ 8
Ⓓ 9

29. Two groups of environmentalists do not agree on the maximum sustainable deer population in a national preserve.

One group states that the deer population can grow according to the function $f(x)=3(1.1)x$ The other group states that the preserve can only support a certain deer population according to the function

$$g(x) = \frac{6}{1 + 0.5e^{-x}}$$

Analyze the function, at $x=2.5$, What does this tell us?

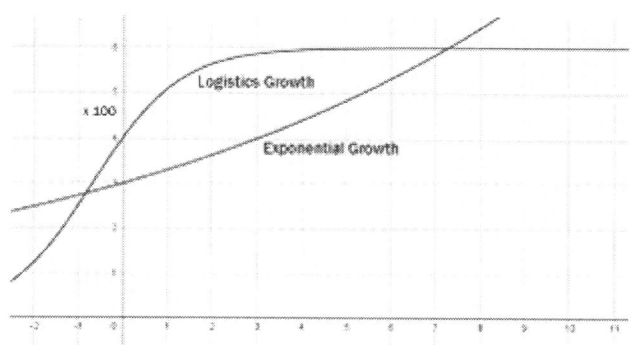

Ⓐ The rates of growth of the deer population is about the same at $x=2.5$
Ⓑ The logistics growth curve is increasing much faster than the exponential growth curve at $x=2.5$
Ⓒ The exponential growth curve is increasing much faster than the logistics growth curve at $x=2.5$
Ⓓ One curve is increasing and the other curve is decreasing at $x=2.5$

30. The number of people entering a stadium, for a concert and pre-concert celebrations, each hour is modeled by $f(t)=27t+38$ where t is the number of hours. During a specific hour, 200 entered the stadium. Which hour was that?

Explain your work in detail.

31. You are tasked to explain the binomial theorem to your study group, using $(2x+7)^2$. What coefficient would you have for the second term in the binomial expansion? Explain how you arrived at the answer.

32. You don't think the absolute value symbol is needed when simplifying the expression $\sqrt[a]{n^a}$ when "a" is an even number.

   You say that the result is always n.

   Which example below does not support your conjecture?

   Ⓐ $\sqrt[5]{7^5} = 7$
   Ⓑ $\sqrt[4]{7^4} = 7$
   Ⓒ $\sqrt[4]{(-7)^4} = 7$
   Ⓓ $\sqrt[4]{(-7)^4} = |-7|$

33. Your friend is looking at some conjugate pairs and she asks you to give the conjugate of the complex number $7-19i$.

   What would you say? Why?

34. A biology professor uses an exponential growth function to discuss the population of fur seals in Antarctica. Is his logic of using this function flawed or logical?

Ⓐ If every male and female fur seal mates successfully, the population will grow exponentially.
Ⓑ An exponential growth function does not consider external factors that can affect population growth.
Ⓒ An exponential growth function correctly shows the population of fur seals.
Ⓓ The population growth of fur seals is linear, not exponential.

35. A classmate of yours stated that a solid line is not a good representation of an arithmetic sequence. What logical assumption is your classmate using?

Ⓐ A line is a series of dots that represents each value of the sequence.
Ⓑ A line has the same slope as the common difference in the sequence.
Ⓒ An arithmetic sequence is a set of discrete values, whereas a line is a continuous set of values.
Ⓓ The classmate is not correct. A line is a good representation of an arithmetic sequence.

36. During a collaborative activity, two students are discussing the population growth of caribou in Alaska displayed in this graph. They are tasked with making a conclusion about the population. Which choice is a likely conclusion they made?

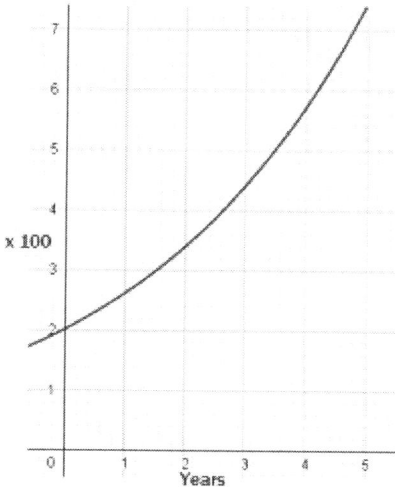

Ⓐ The population will increase until it reaches just over 700
Ⓑ The population will increase more in year 4 than it will increase in year 2
Ⓒ The population is declining.
Ⓓ The population is increasing the same number every year.

Student Name: Start Time:
Test Date: End Time:

Here are some reminders for when you are taking the Practice Test.

To answer the questions on the test, use the directions given in the question. If you do not know the answer to a question, skip it and go on to the next question. If time permits, you may return to questions in this session only. Do your best to answer every question.

Practice Test 2
Performance Task (PT) - 1

Trigonometric Ratios

Find the trigonometric ratios for each of the figures shown. Also, explain how you arrived at the answer.

1. What is the value of the tangent of angle H ?

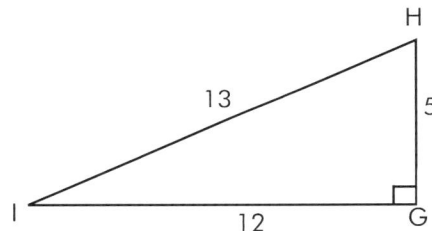

Explain in detail how you arrived at the answer.

1.1 What is the value of the cosecant of \H?

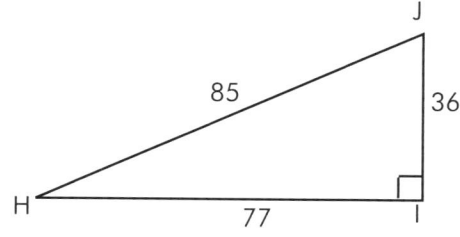

1.2 What is the value of the Secant of \V ?

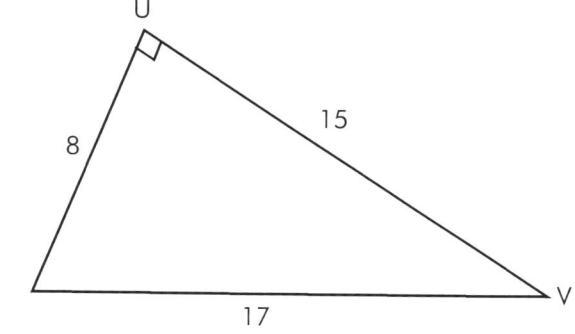

Ⓐ $\frac{17}{15}$

Ⓑ $\frac{8}{15}$

Ⓒ $\frac{15}{17}$

Ⓓ $\frac{17}{18}$

1.3 What is the value of the Cotangent of \X ?

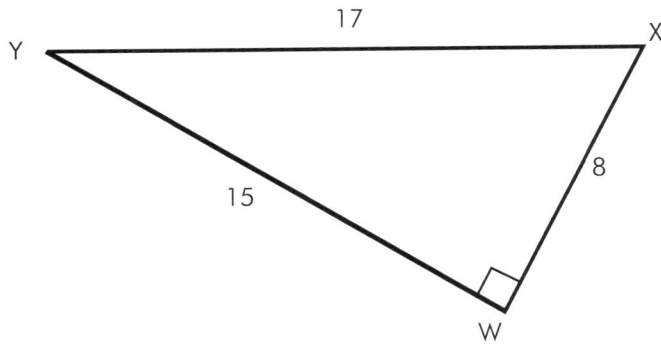

1.4 What is the value of the Sine of \Y?

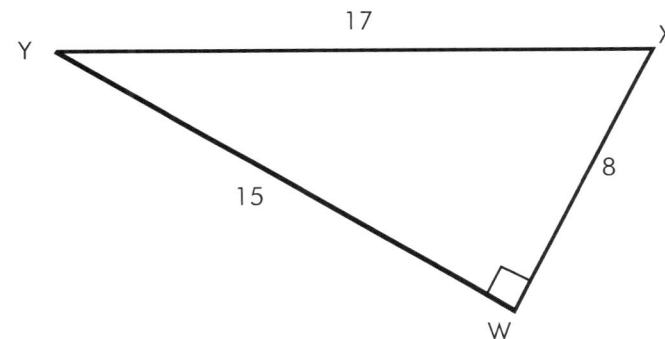

Ⓐ $\frac{8}{17}$

Ⓑ $\frac{17}{8}$

Ⓒ $\frac{15}{8}$

Ⓓ $\frac{17}{15}$

Student Name:
Test Date:

Start Time:
End Time:

Here are some reminders for when you are taking the Practice Test.

To answer the questions on the test, use the directions given in the question. If you do not know the answer to a question, skip it and go on to the next question. If time permits, you may return to questions in this session only. Do your best to answer every question.

Computer Adaptive Test (CAT) - 2

1. What is the coefficient of the first term in the expression $16x^2y^2 - 25$?

   Ⓐ 16
   Ⓑ 25
   Ⓒ -25
   Ⓓ 9

2. Use complete the squares to find the minimum value of : $f(x)=x^2+12x+3$

   Ⓐ 6
   Ⓑ -3
   Ⓒ -33
   Ⓓ -6

3. Which graph shows the solution of $y=\frac{1}{5}x^2 - \frac{4}{5}x - 1$?

   Ⓐ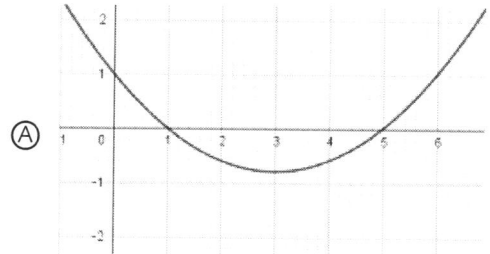

   Ⓑ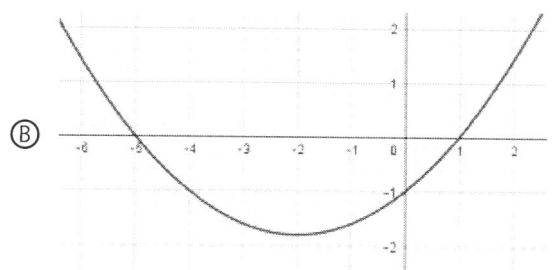

LumosLearning.com

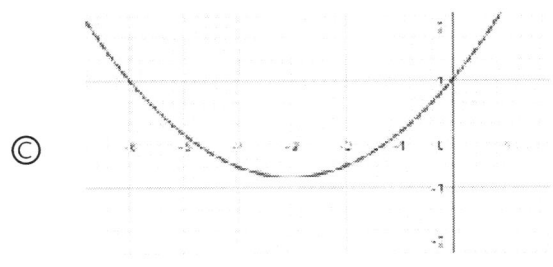

Ⓒ

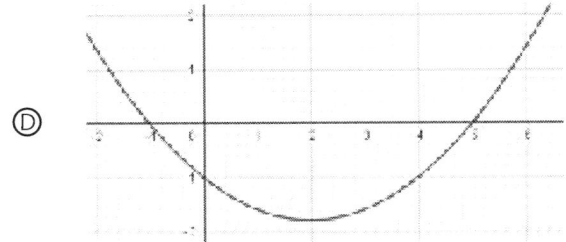

Ⓓ

4. **Which statement is true about the domain and range of a function?**

   Ⓐ The domain is the set of outputs, the range is the set of inputs
   Ⓑ The domain is the set of inputs, the range is the set of outputs
   Ⓒ The range is the set of independent variables, the domain is the set of dependent variables
   Ⓓ The domain is the set of independent variables, the range is the also the set of independent variables

5. **Add these polynomials $(3x^3+4x^2-6x+5)+(x^3-4x^2-3x+4)$**

   Ⓐ $4x^3+9x-9$
   Ⓑ $4x^3-9x+9$
   Ⓒ $2x^3-4x^2-3x$
   Ⓓ $4x^6-9x^2+9$

6. **What is the recursive sequence for the arithmetic sequence shown below?**
   9, 14, 19, 24

   Ⓐ $a_n = a_{n-1} + 6$
   Ⓑ $a_n = a_{n-1} - 5$
   Ⓒ $a_n = a_{n-1} + 5$
   Ⓓ $a_n = 14 + 5(n-1)$

7. What is the recursive sequence for the arithmetic sequence shown below?

   $-3, -15, -75, -375$

   Ⓐ $a_n = a_{n-1} \cdot 3$
   Ⓑ $a_n = a_1 \cdot 3^{n-1}$
   Ⓒ $a_n = a_{n-1} \cdot 5$
   Ⓓ $a_n = a_{n-1} \cdot (-3)$

8. The line graph below shows the number of people at a festival from the time the gate opened until 12 hours later. What does the value 6 represent?
   The x-axis shows "hours since opening" and the y-axis shows "number of people at the festival (hundreds)"

   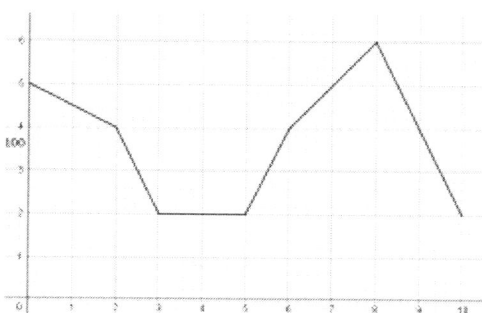

   Ⓐ The maximum number of people at the festival was 600
   Ⓑ The minimum number of people at the festival was 600
   Ⓒ 600 people were at the festival when the gate opened
   Ⓓ 600 people were at the festival when the gate closed

9. The function $f(x) = -\frac{1}{3}(x-6)^2$ is the path of a fly ball at a major league baseball game.

   Its graph is shown below. What is the domain of this function?

   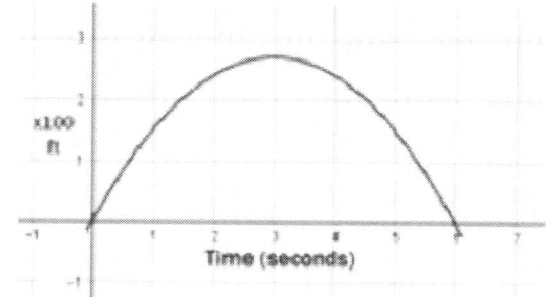

   Ⓐ [6, 0]
   Ⓑ [-1, 7]
   Ⓒ [-∞, ∞]
   Ⓓ [0, 6]

10. Values of a function are given in the table below. What is the average rate of change of the function on the interval [1,11] ?

x	f(x)
-2	4
1	7
5	11
8	8
11	6
14	2

Ⓐ $\frac{-1}{10}$

Ⓑ $\frac{1}{10}$

Ⓒ $\frac{-8}{3}$

Ⓓ $\frac{8}{3}$

11. Write the explicit formula for this geometric sequence: 1,−5,25,−125,.......

Ⓐ $a_n = 1(-5)^n$
Ⓑ $a_n = 1(-5)^{n-1}$
Ⓒ $a_n = 1(5)^n$
Ⓓ $a_n = 1(-5)^{n+1}$

12. Suppose △ABC ~ △DEF shown below. What is tan E?

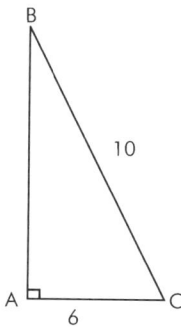 

- Ⓐ $\frac{3}{5}$
- Ⓑ $\frac{4}{3}$
- Ⓒ $\frac{3}{4}$
- Ⓓ $\frac{4}{5}$

13. Suppose

sin angle S = $\frac{3}{5}$ in △RST as shown below. What is the length of $\overline{RS}$?

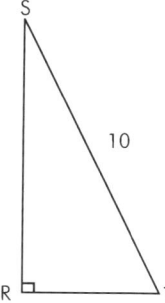

- Ⓐ 8
- Ⓑ 7
- Ⓒ 6
- Ⓓ 9

14. Suppose

sin\S = $\frac{3}{4}$ in △QRS as shown below. What is the length of $\overline{RS}$?

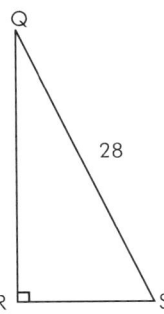

Ⓐ √343
Ⓑ 8.5
Ⓒ √175
Ⓓ 7

15. A survey of students in a class was conducted to record the color of hair each student has. The result of the survey is in the table. What is the probability that a girl has blonde hair?

Hair Color	Boys	Girls	Total
Brown	6	9	15
Black	3	5	8
Red	2	1	3
Blonde	4	6	10
Total	15	21	36

Ⓐ $\frac{2}{7}$

Ⓑ $\frac{7}{12}$

Ⓒ $\frac{3}{5}$

Ⓓ $\frac{4}{15}$

16. Suppose the results of an experiment are plotted on a graph, shown below. What is the relationship between the input and the output of the experiment?

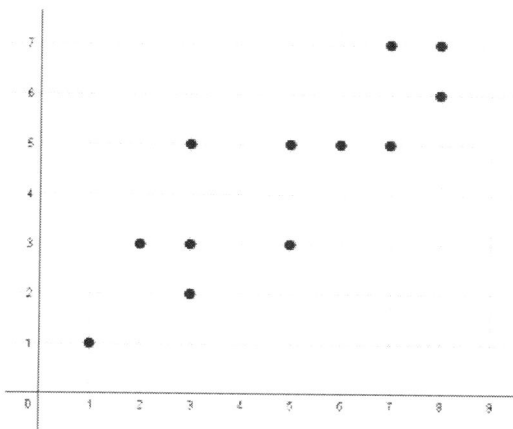

Ⓐ strong positive correlation
Ⓑ weak positive correlation
Ⓒ strong negative correlation
Ⓓ weak negative correlation

17. The union within a company wants its employees to vote for the new pay proposal.

Over a six day period, the following numbers of employees cast their vote :
86, 95, 38, 47, 73, 68

Which number best describes the average number of employee's votes each day?

Ⓐ 63.83
Ⓑ 67.8
Ⓒ 68
Ⓓ 67.83

18. The diameter of a large hydraulic cylinder shaft has a tolerance of 3±0.015 inches.

Which of these answers is within the required tolerance?

Ⓐ 2.8
Ⓑ 2.9
Ⓒ 3.006
Ⓓ 3.02

19. After making repairs, a swimming pool owner is going to refill the pool with water. The pool dimensions are 18x40x6 feet, with each cubic foot equivalent to 2.64 gallons, and the cost of water $0.005 per gallon. To the nearest dollar, what is the estimated cost of filling the pool?

   Ⓐ $11,405
   Ⓑ $57
   Ⓒ $58
   Ⓓ $22

20. Suppose the cost of electricity in Florida is 11.6 cents per kilowatt hour (kWh), and the cost of electricity in Georgia is 10.1 cents per kilowatt hour. What is the difference between electricity costs in Florida and in Georgia if a customer consumes 2,124kWh?

   Ⓐ $246.38
   Ⓑ $31.86
   Ⓒ $214.52
   Ⓓ $460.90

21. The volume formula for a square pyramid is $V=\frac{1}{3}Bh$ where B is the area of the base, and h is the height of the pyramid. What is the height of the pyramid if the volume is 32,400ft³ and the length of one side of the base is 36ft?

   Ⓐ 75ft²
   Ⓑ 125ft
   Ⓒ 75ft
   Ⓓ 225ft

22. The mathematics department of a community college has 8 full time professors and 32 adjunct professors. Each full time professor teaches 6 courses, and each adjunct professor teaches 2 courses. Each course requires an average of 1,350 sheets of paper for duplicating. If the department purchases paper in reams of 5000 sheets, how many reams of paper will the mathematics department purchase?

   Ⓐ 31
   Ⓑ 30
   Ⓒ 29
   Ⓓ 32

23. Suppose the cost of tickets at a county fair is $5 for adults and $3 for children. During the first hour on Saturday, 193 people entered the fair, generating $829 in ticket sales. Use A for adults and C for children. Which system of equations could be used to determine how many adult tickets and how many children tickets were sold?

   Ⓐ 5A + 3C = 829   A + C = 193
   Ⓑ 5A − 3C = 829   A − C = 193
   Ⓒ 5A + 3C = 193   A + C = 829
   Ⓓ A + C = 829   5A + 3C = 193

24. The amount of money in an account is modeled by: $A = 500(1+0.005)^{2t}$

   What is the rate of growth in the account on the interval $3 \leq t \leq 5$

   Answer with a percent and Explain your answer in detail.

25. A small restaurant opened for business and is comparing its projected profit and actual profit for the first year, as shown in the graph below. During which month does the projected profit equal the actual profit?

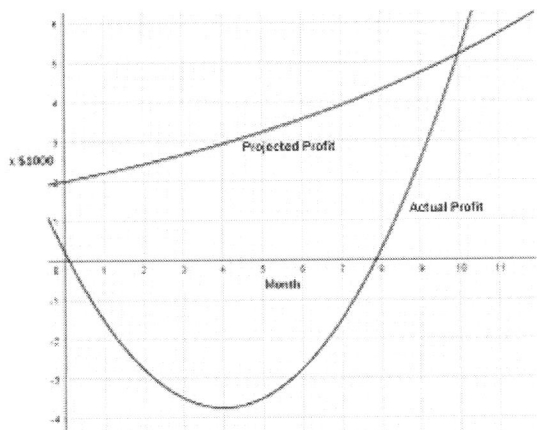

Explain how you arrived at the answer.

26. Given: $15 = 3(2)^{4t}$

Solve for "t" using logarithms. Express your answer to the nearest four decimal places.

Ⓐ 6.9052
Ⓑ 0.5805
Ⓒ 0.9767

27. Given : $24 = 8e^{3t}$

Solve for "t" using logarithms. Express your answer to the nearest four decimal places.

Show the working steps to arrive at the answer.

28. A preserved plant contains 10 micrograms (10 millionths of a gram) of Carbon-14. The amount of Carbon-14 present in the preserved plant is modeled by the model

$$f(t) = A\left(\frac{1}{2}\right)^{\frac{t}{5370}}$$

Where t denotes time in years since the death of the plant and A is the amount of Carbon-14 present in the plant when it died, measured in micrograms. How many micrograms of Carbon-14 were present in the living plant if it died 1000 years ago? Round your answer to the nearest four decimal places.

29. Juan's father is measuring the distance from his home to his work site with his car. What is the most logical distance for him to use?

Ⓐ 59,136 feet
Ⓑ 19,712 yards
Ⓒ 11.2 miles
Ⓓ 18.025 meter

30. Jackie said that if three numbers are labeled a, b and c the equation $a^2+b^2=c^2$ is always true. Which choice disproves Jackie's conjecture?

Ⓐ a= 6, b= 8, c= 10
Ⓑ a= $\sqrt{5}$, b= $\sqrt{17}$, c=$\sqrt{22}$
Ⓒ a=$3\sqrt{2}$, b=$4\sqrt{3}$, c=$12\sqrt{6}$
Ⓓ a=5, b=12, c=13

31. Dianna states that the sine of an acute angle is equal to the cosine of the complement of that same acute angle. Which choice proves Dianna's conjecture?

Ⓐ $\sin 45° = \frac{\sqrt{2}}{2}, \cos 45° = \frac{\sqrt{2}}{2}$

Ⓑ $\sin 60° = -\frac{\sqrt{3}}{2}, \cos 30° = -\frac{\sqrt{3}}{2}$

Ⓒ $\sin 75° = 0.9659, \cos 25° = 0.9659$

Ⓓ $\sin 65° = 0.9630, \cos 25° = 0.9630$

32. Ms. Peterson, an algebra teacher, told her students that the sum of three consecutive odd integers is always another odd integer. Which choice supports her conjecture?

Ⓐ $x+(x+1)+(x+2)=3x+3$
Ⓑ $x+(x+2)+(x+4)=3x+6$
Ⓒ $x+(2x)+(2x)=5x$
Ⓓ $x+(x+4)(x+8)=3x+12$

33. When solving an exponential equation, we must convert the exponential equation to a logarithmic equation. Which process correctly converts the exponential equation $26=4(3)^{2x}$ to a logarithmic equation?

    Ⓐ $\log 26 = 2x\log[4(3)]$
    Ⓑ $\log \frac{26}{4} = 2x\log 3$
    Ⓒ $26 = 8x\log 3$
    Ⓓ $\log 26 = 4x\log 3^2$

34. You are tasked to prove that the values of y in the equation $7x-y=5$ change by the same amount in every interval of the same length. You decide to identify some intervals you could use for this proof. Which interval should not be used?

    Ⓐ [0,2]
    Ⓑ [15,17]
    Ⓒ [6,8]
    Ⓓ [7,10]

35. Maria and Gorvick are comparing investment options for their vacation account. They see one option that compounds the interest annually. Based on their initial investment of $1000, they anticipate an account balance shown in the table below.

Year	Balance
3	$1,061.21
5	$1,104.08

    A friend of theirs tells them they could earn more interest if the interest was compounded more often, even if the interest rate is the same. Which option compounds the most often?

    Ⓐ $A = 1000\left(1 + \frac{0.05}{12}\right)^{12t}$

    Ⓑ $A = 1000\left(1 + \frac{0.05}{2}\right)^{2t}$

    Ⓒ $A = 1000\left(1 + \frac{0.05}{52}\right)^{52t}$

    Ⓓ $A = 1000\left(1 + \frac{0.05}{4}\right)^{4t}$

LumosLearning.com

36. **A musician's journal used the sine curve to model the vibrations of a tuning fork. Why does this curve violate logic?**

Ⓐ The sine curve shows a never ending vibration that goes on forever.
Ⓑ The sine curve shows the tuning fork vibrating in both directions.
Ⓒ The sine curve shows the tuning fork passing through the origin.
Ⓓ The sine curve shows the tuning fork vibrating at a constant speed.

Additional Information

Test Taking Tips

1) **The day before the test,** make sure you get a good night's sleep.

2) **On the day of the test,** be sure to eat a good hearty breakfast! Also, be sure to arrive at school on time.

3) **During the test:**

- **Read every question carefully.**
    - Do not spend too much time on any one question. Work steadily through all questions in the section.
    - Attempt all of the questions even if you are not sure of some answers.
    - If you run into a difficult question, eliminate as many choices as you can and then pick the best one from the remaining choices. Intelligent guessing will help you increase your score.
    - Also, mark the question so that if you have extra time, you can return to it after you reach the end of the section.
    - Some questions may refer to a graph, chart, or other kind of picture. Carefully review the graphic before answering the question.
    - Be sure to include explanations for your written responses and show all work.

- **While Answering Multiple-Choice (EBSR) questions.**
    - Select the bubble corresponding to your answer choice.
    - Read **all** of the answer choices, even if think you have found the correct answer.

- **While Answering TECR questions.**
    - Read the directions of each question. Some might ask you to drag something, others to select, and still others to highlight. Follow all instructions of the question (or questions if it is in multiple parts)

Other High School Resources

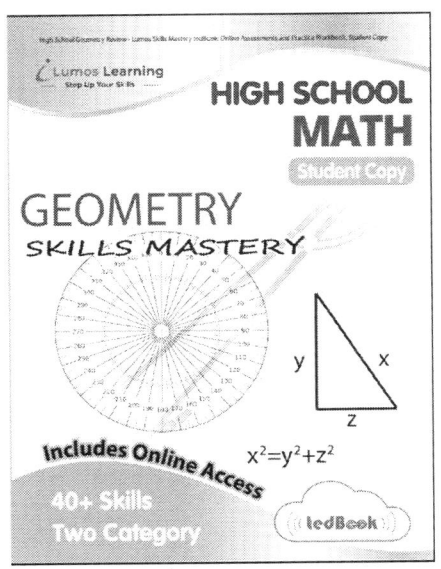

Available
- At Leading book stores
- Online www.LumosLearning.com

Made in the USA
Middletown, DE
03 April 2025

73600353R00024